Breaking the Sound Barrier

by Vickey Herold

Table of Contents

Introduction	2
Chapter 1 What Is the Sound Barrier?	4
Chapter 2 How Did People Break the Sound Barrier?	8
Chapter 3 Why Was Breaking the Sound Barrier Important?	16
Summary	20
Glossary	22
Index	24

Introduction

People wanted airplanes to fly faster. Some people said the **sound barrier** stopped airplanes. Then people built better airplanes. People built airplanes to fly faster than sound.

Words to Know

 engine

 flights

 pilots

 rocket

 scientists

 sound barrier

 space

 speed

 supersonic

▲ People wanted faster airplanes.

See the Glossary on page 22.

Chapter 1

What Is the Sound Barrier?

The sound barrier happens at a **speed**. The sound barrier happens at 760 miles per hour (1,223 kilometers per hour). People learned about the sound barrier. People learned when they flew airplanes.

▲ People learned when airplanes flew.

Solve This

The speed of sound changes at different temperatures. Look at the graphs. How does temperature change the speed of sound?

Answer: Sound travels faster in higher temperatures.

Temperature	Speed of Sound
60°F	762 miles per hour
40°F	747 miles per hour
20°F	732 miles per hour

Temperature	Speed of Sound
16°C	1,226 kilometers per hour
4°C	1,202 kilometers per hour
-7°C	1,178 kilometers per hour

Pilots tried to fly near the speed of sound. The airplanes began to shake. Pilots lost control. The airplanes often crashed.

▲ **Airplanes often crashed.**

It's a Fact

People knew about the speed of sound. Sir Isaac Newton wrote about the speed of sound. The year was 1687.

Chapter 1

People said the sound barrier happened at very fast speeds. People said airplanes could not fly so fast. People said airplanes could not break the sound barrier.

sound barrier

▲ **People said airplanes could not break the sound barrier.**

What Is the Sound Barrier?

Some people wanted to fly faster. People needed better airplanes. People needed airplanes to fly faster than sound.

▲ People needed faster airplanes.

Reread
Reread pages 4–7. Why did people want to break the sound barrier?

Chapter 2

How Did People Break the Sound Barrier?

Chuck Yeager was a pilot. Yeager was in the United States Air Force. Yeager broke the sound barrier on October 14, 1947. Yeager flew an airplane faster than sound.

▲ Chuck Yeager broke the sound barrier.

People tried to break the sound barrier. People tried before 1947. Airplanes often crashed at the speed of sound. Airplanes did not fly through the sound barrier safely.

▲ The sound barrier caused airplanes to crash.

Chapter 2

People wanted to make new types of airplanes. People wanted airplanes to go faster than sound. People knew that bullets go faster than sound.

▲ Some people said airplanes could break the sound barrier.

How Did People Break the Sound Barrier?

Then people made a new type of airplane. The airplane was the Bell X-1.

▲ People made a new type of airplane.

The airplane had the shape of a bullet.

▲ The Bell X-1 was the shape of a bullet.

Try This

1. Fold a paper airplane pointed like a bullet.

2. Fold another paper airplane. Do not make this airplane pointed.

Which one flies faster?

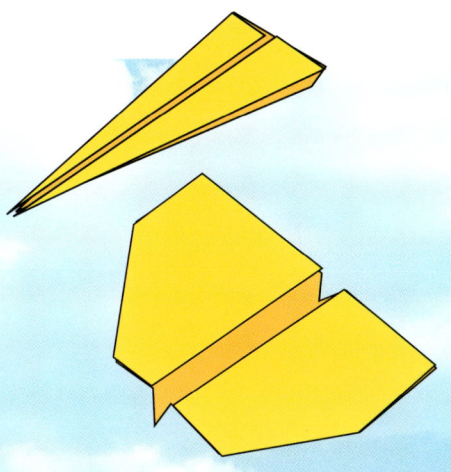

Chapter 2

Chuck Yeager was the pilot of the Bell X-1. The Bell X-1 had a **rocket engine**. The Bell X-1 was the first **supersonic** airplane.

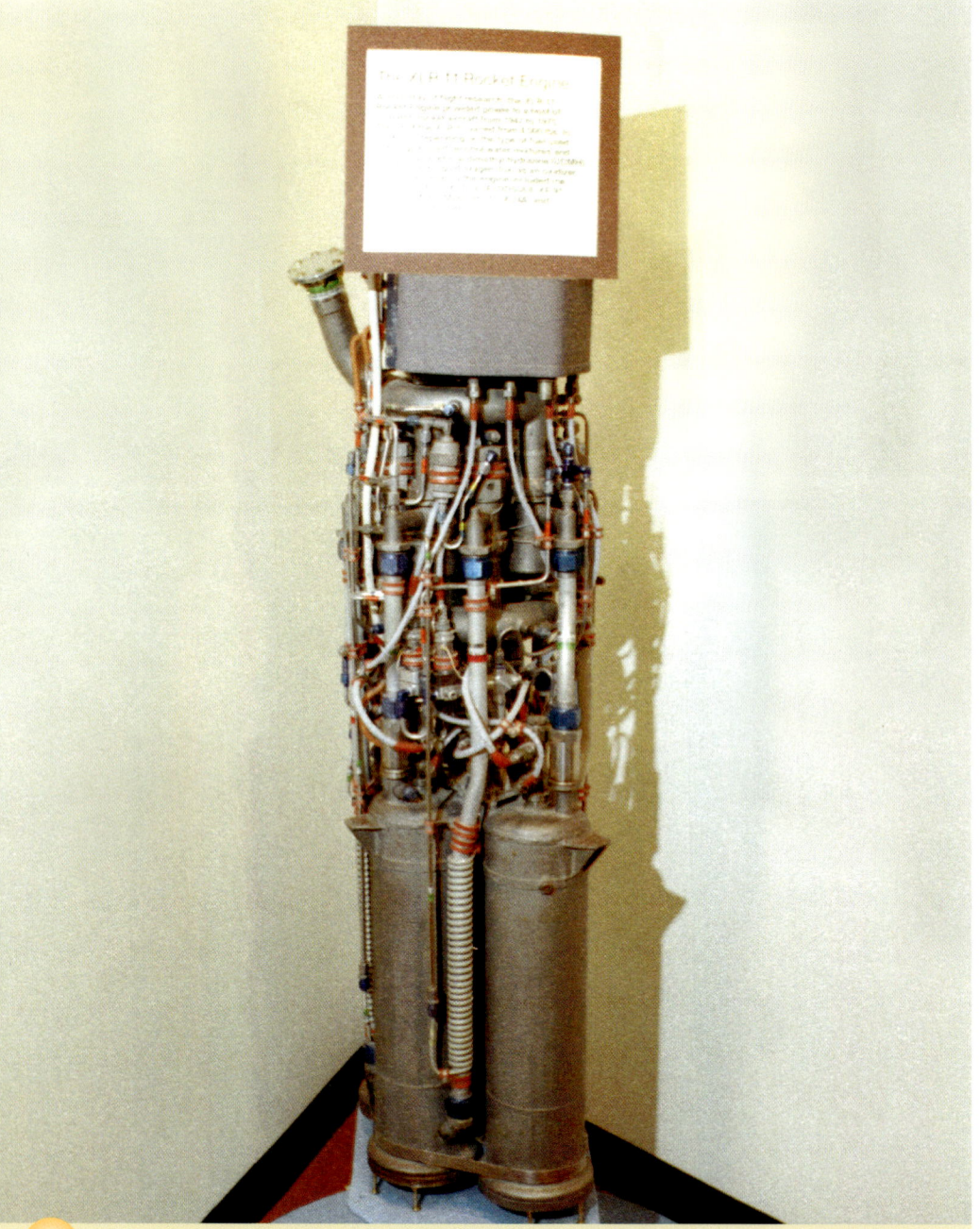

▲ The Bell X-1 had a rocket engine.

How Did People Break the Sound Barrier?

Yeager made nine **flights** in 1947. The flights were very dangerous. No one knew what might happen.

▲ The Bell X-1 went very fast.

Did You Know?
Yeager fell two days before his famous flight. Yeager broke two ribs. He did not tell anyone about the accident. He wanted to fly the airplane.

13

Chapter 2

The flight on October 14, 1947, was successful. Yeager flew faster than the speed of sound. The Bell X-1 did not crash. Today airplanes fly faster than the speed of sound.

▲ Airplanes fly faster than the speed of sound.

It's a Fact

People heard a sonic boom. A sonic boom is a very loud noise. The boom happened when Yeager broke the sound barrier. Sonic booms happen when airplanes break the sound barrier.

How Did People Break the Sound Barrier?

Chuck Yeager became famous. Yeager became a general in the United States Air Force. People say Chuck Yeager is an American hero.

Did You Know?
Jacqueline Cochran broke the sound barrier in 1953. Now many women pilots fly faster than sound.

▲ People say Chuck Yeager is an American hero.

Chapter 3

Why Was Breaking the Sound Barrier Important?

Breaking the sound barrier helped **scientists**. Scientists learned new things about sound. Scientists learned new things about speed.

▲ Scientists learned many new things.

Today scientists build many supersonic airplanes. Supersonic airplanes fly faster than sound. Supersonic airplanes fly safely through the sound barrier.

▲ Today scientists build supersonic airplanes.

Chapter 3

Air travel is better today. Airplanes fly more. Airplanes fly faster. Airplanes fly safely at supersonic speeds.

▲ Airplanes fly safely at supersonic speeds today.

It's a Fact

People built a supersonic airplane in the 1960s. The Concorde was a very large airplane. The Concorde went faster than the speed of sound. The Concorde went two times the speed of sound. The Concorde stopped flying in 2003.

Why Was Breaking the Sound Barrier Important?

Breaking the sound barrier helped scientists learn other things. Scientists learned more about building rockets.

▲ Scientists built rockets.

Scientists learned more about **space** travel.

Did You Know?

Chuck Yeager helped people go into space. Yeager started the school that teaches astronauts. Yeager started the school in 1962.

▲ Breaking the sound barrier helped people go into space.

Summary

Airplanes did not break the sound barrier at first. Then people made airplanes that flew faster. Chuck Yeager broke the sound barrier first. Today many people fly faster than sound.

What Is the Sound Barrier?
- happens at very fast speeds
- 760 miles per hour (1,223 kilometers per hour)
- was the fastest speed for airplanes

Breaking the Sound Barrier

How Did People Break the Sound Barrier?
- had faster airplane
- Bell X-1
- rocket engine
- supersonic airplane

Why Was Breaking the Sound Barrier Important?

taught scientists new things
helped scientists build supersonic airplanes
made air travel better
airplanes fly faster
taught scientists about space travel

Think About It

1. What is the sound barrier?
2. How did Chuck Yeager break the sound barrier?
3. Why was breaking the sound barrier important?

Glossary

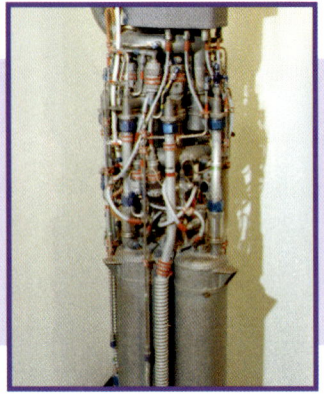

engine a machine that moves energy

The Bell X-1 had a rocket engine.

flights airplane travels

Yeager made nine flights in 1947.

pilots people who fly airplanes

Pilots lost control.

rocket something that moves by power from behind

The Bell X-1 had a rocket engine.

scientists people who study science

Scientists learned new things about sound.

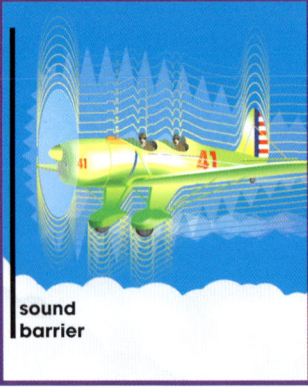

sound barrier an air speed of 760 miles per hour (1,223 kilometers per hour)

Some people said the sound barrier stopped airplanes.

22

space the region beyond Earth

*Scientists learned more about **space** travel.*

speed how fast something moves

*The sound barrier happens at a **speed**.*

supersonic faster than the speed of sound

*The Bell X-1 was the first **supersonic** airplane.*

Index

airplanes, 2, 4–12, 14, 17–18, 20

Bell X-1, 11–12, 14

bullets, 10–11

engine, 12

flights, 13–14

general, 15

hero, 15

pilots, 5, 8, 12

rocket, 12, 19

scientists, 16–17, 19

sound barrier, 2, 4, 6, 8–9, 16–17, 19–20

space, 19

speed, 4, 16, 18

speed of sound, 5, 9, 14

supersonic, 12, 17–18

United States Air Force, 8, 15

Yeager, Chuck, 8, 12–15, 20